They that hope in the Lord,
will renew their strength,
they will soar as with eagles' wings,
they will run and not grow weary,
walk and not grow faint.

Isaiah 40:31

Salesian Missions wishes to extend special thanks and gratitude to our generous poet friends and to the publishers who have given us permission to reprint material included in this book. Every effort has been made to give proper acknowledgments. Any omissions or errors are deeply regretted, and the publisher, upon notification, will be pleased to make the necessary corrections in subsequent editions.

First Edition Printed in the U.S.A. by Concord Litho Co., Inc., Concord, New Hampshire 03301-0464

The Shelter of His Wings

from the Salesian Collection

Compiled and edited by
Sara Tarascio

Illustrated by
Paul Scully, Frank Massa,
Dorian Lee Remine
and
Russell Bushée

Contents

I am the Good Shepherd 6
He Leadeth Me 7
No Secret Hiding Place 8
It's the Thought That Counts ..9
Talk to Him 10
A Door is Closed 12
We All Need a Dream 13
My Blessed Home 14
The Little Hummingbird 15
By Day and Night 16
Plant a Seed 18
Each New Dawning Day 19
A Symphonic Moment............20
Forever Friends 21
A Lovely Day............................22
His Peace 24
Living Waters 25
Sing with Thanksgiving! 26
The Measure of a Man............27
Faith 28
Life Is Worth Living 29
As Eagles 30
An Eagle with a Broken Wing 31
We give thanks to You 32
He's Always Been That Way ..33
All That's Needed Is a Heart..34
Lack of Faith 35
I Have No Worries 36
The Guardian 37
Peace..38
In Perfect Harmony 39
Hang Gliding 40
All of Me 41
Thanksgiving Day in the Country 42
Sunshine in My Heart 44
God's Majesty..........................45
The Prayer Flower 46
Quietude 47
For a Brand-New Day 48
Smile 49
The Lord is my light 50
We Can't . . . but God Can! 51
Leave Everything in God's Hands........................52
Seasons of Life........................54
The Source of Every Blessing 55
It Will Always Be Amazing 56
A Faith Is Mine........................58
God, Show Me How................59
With Sled in Tow 60
Prayer for Strength..................61
Innocence 62
Faith Produces Works 63
Growing in Grace 64
Keep the Faith 65
Shelter Us 66
God's Rebel Rose....................67
Texture of My Soul..................68

Nobody's Perfect 69
Early Spring 70
It's April...................................71
The Journey Home 72
Slow Me Down 73
God's Gift of Memory 74
A Wealth of Memories............75
One Little Stray 76
World of Chapels 77
Treasures I Hold Dear 78
The Ecstasies of Spring..........79
Home and Hearth 80
Time for God............................81
Cabin of My Dreams 82
If Memories Are Riches..........84
I Thank God for My Home......85
Holy Is His Name....................86
Time for Change......................87
I Offer Thanks 88
Lack of Knowledge..................89
The Little Horse
Who Failed..........................90
Admonition 91
Then Jesus Approached..........92
The Great Commission 93
After the Winter, God
Sends the Spring................94
Get Away from All of It 95
Autumn 96
Set Me Afire 97
A Day Worthwhile 98
My Daily Prayer 99
Gentle Folk 100
The Secret.............................101
The Heralds of Spring 102
Snow Picnic 103
Beside the Waters 104
Beware the Seed 106
The Faith of a
Mustard Seed...................107
Not by Chance nor
Happenstance 108
A New Beginning 110
The Spring 111
The Glory of life 112
The Eagle 113
Dear Friend 114
Before the Dawn of Day 115
At the End of the Tunnel......116
February Contentment 118
Beyond the Winter...............119
Beyond the Clouds 120
A Fond Farewell 122
Retreat 123
When You Kneel to Pray 124
The Eagle's Flight.................125
Lonesome.............................126
Listening Ears 127
Ask Not What God Can
Do for You 128

I am the Good Shepherd:
the Good Shepherd giveth
his life for his sheep.
John 10:11

He Leadeth Me

He leadeth me across the years,
I watch each one depart,
Filled with a gladness when I see
His footprints on my heart.
I place my hand within His own
And feel that I have wings,
He's given me the rainbow
And now a soul that sings.

He leadeth me down every path,
And I am not afraid,
He loves me, even knowing
The mistakes that I have made.
He teaches me what pure delight
We find the more we give
And that to be unselfish,
Is the only way to live.

He leadeth me from dawn to dusk,
As seasons come and go,
He is my guide to inner peace
And everything I know.
A little shadow of Himself
Is what I've come to be,
Always safe and warm because
. . . The dear Lord leadeth me!

Grace E. Easley

*He restoreth my soul:
He leadeth me in the
paths of righteousness
for His name's sake.*
Ps. 23:3

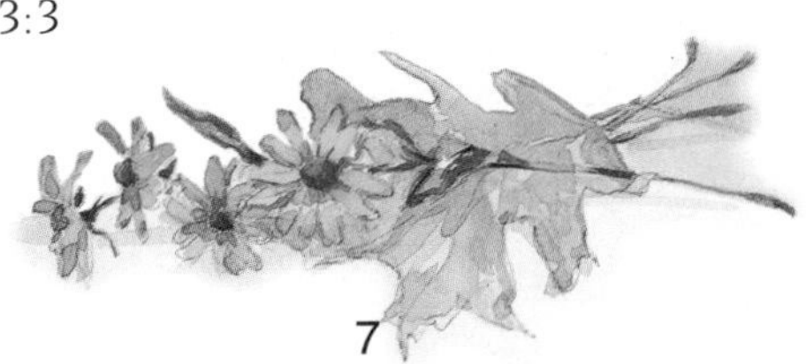

No Secret Hiding Place

Wherever we go, whatever we do
We cannot go beyond God's view.
There is no secret hiding place
Where He'll not look upon our face,
And we must ever strive to be
The Christian that He wants to see.
To love and serve Him every day
And help someone to find the way.
Lest we would hang our heads in shame -
For someday He will call our name.

Kay Hoffman

In You Lord
I take refuge;
let me never
be put to shame . . .
Ps. 31:2

It's the Thought That Counts

Often in times of trouble
we don't know what to say,
So we choose to say nothing,
and sometimes run away.
When friends are really hurting,
we don't know what to do,
So we offer weak excuses
or say we're hurting, too.

It really doesn't matter
what kind of gift we bring;
We only need to be there
if we don't bring a thing.
It truly is amazing
what a hug can do,
When heartache numbs the senses,
and friends depend on you.

There's comfort just in knowing
that you are not alone,
When tears are overflowing,
and hearts are cold as stone.
It's the loving prayers of others
that balance our accounts,
For when we measure love,
it's still the thought that counts.

Clay Harrison

Talk to Him

Talk to Him, soon as you open your eyes,
Thank Him for every new day,
Tell Him you love Him, throughout every hour,
Don't be too busy to pray.
Tell Him good night, when you lie down
to sleep,
Ask His forgiveness if there
Is something you feel that you shouldn't
have done,
Go to Him often in prayer.

Talk to Him, make Him a part of your life,
Include Him in all that you do,
He knows the heartaches you've learned how to hide,
The things you are going through.
He knows all your questions, but better than that,
He has the solutions, too. . .
So talk to the Lord, and know in your heart,
. . . He's waiting to talk to you!

Grace E. Easley

May your ear be attentive and your eyes open, to heed the prayer which I now offer . . .
Neh. 1:6

A Door is Closed

A door is closed and locked behind
Me at each end of day
And I can't open it, nor tread
Again along that way.

It has a window small, and I
Can peer through it awhile,
But then my vision dimmer gets
As I walk each new mile.

So I suppose it's best by far
To keep my eyes ahead,
Forget the past and live each day
A better life instead.

Luther Elvis Albright

*"I am the door: by Me,
if any man enter in,
he shall be saved,
and shall go in and go out
and shall find pasture.*
John 10:9

We All Need a Dream

We all need a dream for tomorrow,
A goal to strive to attain,
A dream for a better tomorrow
Where love might truly reign.
For God put us here for a purpose;
Let us not stand idly by,
But fasten our dream to a rainbow
And for its fulfillment strive.

Dreams are like stars in the heavens
Which seem, oh, so faraway;
Yet, let not these dreams elude us
But keep them alive each day.
We all need a dream to master,
A dream to gladden the heart,
A dream that will help make better
God's world . . . of which we're a part.

Loise Pinkerton Fritz

That ye might walk worthy of the Lord unto all pleasing, being fruitful in every good work, and increasing the knowledge of God.
Col. 1:10

My Blessed Home

I don't have to go to the rolling hills
To sense the joys of nature's thrills.
From my front porch I see fine trees
And hear the songs of wind and leaves.
I listen to the hum of flies
And watch the ever-changing skies.
I sense the quiet of the day
And hear the children near at play.
I lay relaxed upon this chair
And dream and think in silent prayer.
There is no urge to want to roam
For blessed is my home sweet home.

Tee Lowrey

*Every good gift
and every perfect
gift is from above . . .*
James 1:17

The Little Hummingbird

I was weeding flowers
When I heard a little sound
Of something which was in distress,
And when I looked around,
I saw a tiny hummingbird,
Securely caught within
A spider's web, and quickly
Reached up to rescue him.
What a gigantic spider
Slid down to claim his prey
And just in time I snatched
The frightened hummingbird away.
It did not struggle in my hand,
Which held it carefully
And I could tell within its eyes,
The small one trusted me.
So I removed the spider's
Sticky web from little wings,
And marveled at the beauty
God bestows on tiny things.
And then it cocked its little head
And gave me one last stare,
Circled once above my head,
. . . And flew into the air.

Grace E. Easley

By Day and Night

I walk with Him, Who walks with me
In darkness and in light
And is companion to my trials
And savior to my frights;
He never leaves me to the fates
That come of life's despairs
And never lets me bear, alone,
The burdens I must bear.

No matter which of paths I trod -
Or where I chance to be -
He walks along, to share my fates,
And watches over me;
And - when I stumble, fall or cry,
Or dread some fretful way -
He's always near, to dry my tears
And comfort my dismay.

By day and night, He walks with me
And never curbs my wills;
And every joy, that tempts my heart,
He grants me to fulfill
But - when I do some wrongful deed
That taints my soul with sin -
He pricks my conscience, with a twinge,
To make amends to Him.

And so we walk, alone and one,
My Gracious Lord and me -
A silent Spirit, by my side,
I never hear or see -
But I'm aware that He is there,
And sees the deeds I do,
And will be judge of everyone -
When life, on earth, is through.

Michael Dubina

Plant a Seed

Plant a seed, then watch it grow
In your garden row on row,
Midst rain and sunshine you shall see
The miracle bright and free.

Plant a seed and tend it well
Neath the soil where wonders dwell,
Soon your eyes shall fondly see
A plant that's growing patiently.

Trust in nature and you'll find
Even clouds are silver lined,
Miracles from out the sod,
Plant a seed and trust in God.

Garnett Ann Schultz

Behold, God is my salvation;
I will trust, and not be afraid.
Is. 12:2

Each New Dawning Day

Do not lose hope nor faith my friend,
Tho heartsick you may be.
This world is filled with pleasant things,
That now you cannot see.

The tears that well within your eyes
May dim the sunshine bright,
But luck is bound to change for you,
As day must follow night.

We all have had such moments
And felt the same as you,
But in the end we always found
The sun came shining thru.

Throw off your feeling of despair
And brush those tears away . . .
Your world will be a brighter place
With each new dawning day.

Harold F. Mohn

The night is passed, and the day is at hand. Let us therefore cast off the works of darkness, and put on the armour of light.
Rom. 13:12

A Symphonic Moment

Come listen to the ocean's song
And hear a symphony,
Concordance keyed to merging notes,
A tidal ecstasy.

A dot of time when earth and sky
Unite upon the shore;
Full complement of nature's best,
Oh hear the crash and roar.

But waves becalm, then disappear
Into a softened night;
And with the steps of slowed retreat
The music takes its flight.

And standing there I sense my loss
As trailing notes fade low;
From sea to sea - God's symphony,
As throbbing ebb and flow.

Henry W. Gurley

Forever Friends

I love the rhythm of the waves
That ebb and flood upon the sand,
As constant as the TLC
That we receive from God's own hand.

He's there for us each time we call
On Him in times of deep despair,
To give us strength to carry on
When we feel that no one will care.

He's there to celebrate with us
When joy attempts to burst our seams;
He is the friend who's always there
Encouraging our hopes and dreams.

He's there when we are feeling sad,
Caught up in worries of the day -
Yes, God is there when e'er we ask,
If we but take the time to pray.

He's there to share each joy and tear -
The best friend you shall ever know.
There is no soul God does not love
If only you will to Him go.

Yes, like the waves that endlessly
Flow rhythmically upon the shore,
God's love is for eternity;
He'll be your friend forevermore.

Sandra Town Lytle

A Lovely Day

Today I watched the sun creep up
Behind the distant hills,
I listened to the symphony
Of birds resound their trills.
They seemed to greet this brand-new day
With praise to God above,
And in the stillness I knelt down
To thank Him for His love.

I took time from my chores today
To walk a country way
Where April burst with glory
In a magnificent display.
I watched the meadow flowers dance
A rainbow Spring ballet,
And there my soul was filled with peace
As worries slipped away.

I saw a child upon a swing
Whose face was wet with tears.
Her dolly had a broken arm -
I tried to calm her fears.
A broken doll and heart to mend
Were not just what I planned,
But oh, to see her happy smile
Made my day extra grand.

I bought some flowers at a stand,
A pretty, bright bouquet,
I gave them to a shut-in friend
Who said it "made her day."
God's presence seemed to fill my heart
Each step along the way.
I found such joy in simple things -
It was a lovely day!

Beverly J. Anderson

His Peace

You may have a burden;
you may have a care.
You may find your troubles
are too much to bear.
But there is a peace
beyond understanding -
Not as the world knows,
but within your commanding.

The Lord said, "My peace
I will give unto you.
Receive Me in faith;
that's all you need do.
Let your heart not be troubled;
let it not be afraid.
The peace I give you
will never fade."

Barbara A. McDowell

John 14:27

Living Waters

God's Love is like
A shining stream
That overflows
With golden beams.
It enters in
Our hearts with light,
And pours out blessings
Day or night.

This living stream
Can cleanse from sin
Those hearts that bid
It enter in.
Its flowing spirit
Endlessly
Is bringing Christ
To you and me.

Amy C. Ellis

Sing with Thanksgiving!

Keep a happy song in your heart
- Wherever you may go -
And sing it out in praise to God,
Then feel the blessings flow!

Our God is pleased when we sing praise
And offer Him our love -
So He will bless our hearts with joy,
And comfort from above.

Think of the peace He offers you
Through the privilege of prayer -
And how He's always near to you
To show how much He cares.

Consider the world He's given us
- With plants and birds and trees -
There's so much to be thankful for!
We should be on our knees...

So sing with thanksgiving in your heart
For all that God has done -
And thank Him most especially...
For Jesus Christ, His Son!

Denise A. DeWald

"The Lord is my strength and my shield;
my heart trusts in Him, and I am helped.
My heart leaps for joy and
I will give thanks to Him in song."
Ps. 28:7

The Measure of a Man

He is not poor who has a friend
to share his sorrow till the end,
Who daily does some little thing
that tends to make a sad heart sing.

He is not poor who gives away
the gift of laughter every day,
Who shares the pain and yet can smile
because He knows that life's worthwhile.

He is not poor who dares to fight
for what he feels is true and right...
The unsung hero, at his best,
the unknown soldier laid to rest.

He is not poor who does these things
Although he has no diamond rings,
Because his wealth is stored above
and measured by God's staff of love.

Clay Harrison

Faith

I will not doubt, though all my ships at sea
Come drifting home with broken masts and sails;
I shall believe the Hand which never fails,
From seeming evil worketh good to me;
And, though I weep because those sails are battered,
Still will I cry, while my best hopes lie shattered,
"I trust in Thee."

I will not doubt; well anchored in the faith,
Like some stanch ship, my soul braves every gale,
So strong its courage that it will not fail
To breast the mighty, unknown sea of death.
Oh, may I cry when body parts with spirit,
"I do not doubt," so listening worlds may hear it
With my last breath.

Ella Wheeler Wilcox

Life Is Worth Living

When you feel so alone and empty,
And life seems hopeless and vain,
Your problems are too much to handle,
And your teardrops are falling like rain...
You wish there was someone to help you,
But you don't want to bother your friends,
And you don't want to burden your family,
So you struggle with whatever life sends.

If you lift your eyes up toward Heaven
And you seek for God's goodness and grace,
He'll remove the sorrow you carry,
Send contentment and peace in its place.
He'll give you joy and assurance:
There's no limit to His giving,
When you seek God and you find Him,
Then your life will be worth living.

Frances Culp Wolfe

As Eagles

Our God is never weary.
He's always standing near,
Empowering us to conquer
Our problems and our fear.
In Him just keep on trusting,
On Him our faith must rest,
When we wait upon the Lord
Our strength is at its best.
He gives us power in weakness,
He helps us run the race,
Anything is possible
When covered by His grace.
We'll run and not be weary.
He shall our strength renew,
Replenished by His Spirit,
We soar as eagles do.

Martha Mastin

You have seen what I have done to the Egyptians, how I have carried you upon the wings of eagles and brought you to myself.
Exod. 19:4

An Eagle with a Broken Wing

Like an eagle with a broken wing,
I cannot soar above,
For I am grounded by my fate -
a prisoner of love.
I did not choose the path I trod
for heavy is the load,
But I have faith and trust my God
to help me down the road.
I must take the "road less traveled"
to do my Master's will,
And bear the thorn within my side
which leads to Calvary's hill.
Now I must follow in His steps
because He first chose me
Like an eagle with a broken wing
striving to breathe free.

Clay Harrison

But they that hope in the
Lord shall renew their strength,
they shall mount up with wings as eagles . . .
Isai. 40:31

We give thanks to You, O God. We call upon Your name and declare Your wonderful works.

Ps. 75:1

He's Always Been That Way

He knows my needs before I do,
He's always been that way,
He walks before me just to clear
The stones out of the way.
He hears my faintest whisper,
And sees my smallest tear,
And He tells me there's a reason
As to why He put me here.

He knows my faults and failings,
And the times that I complain,
My trials and tribulations,
And the plans that were in vain.
But He says this doesn't matter,
And it all will pass away,
That I've only but to trust Him
For He made me out of clay.

So I take the bits and pieces,
Of this life I've come to know,
And I tell Him "All for Jesus,"
. . . As I did so long ago,
And I feel my burden lifted,
And I know that come what may,
His love for me is endless,
And He's always been that way!

Grace E. Easley

But strive first the kingdom of God and His *righteousness and all these things will be given to you as well.*
Matt. 6:33

All That's Needed Is a Heart

You need not be of wealth or fame,
Nor excel in works of art
To improve the world around you -
All that's needed is a heart.

You need not be a wise man
To know how you can mend
Another's broken spirit,
As a helping hand you lend.

You need not be a fiddler
To keep one's heart in tune
With a happy melody,
Though dreams may lie in ruin.

And a lesson in futility
You'll need never know,
As you trust God as your Mentor
And to your life's calling go.

Catherine Janssen Irwin

Lack of Faith

Why do we keep on falling
And never find the way
That holds the peace and joys of life
For which we plead and pray;
Is it because we lack the faith
To trust unto the Lord
And offer Him just empty prayers,
In hopes of some reward;
And is this why He lets us fall
To suffer varied fates -
Because He sees our doubting hearts
And lack of trust and faith?
I'm sure it is - and also sure -
He waits to hear our prayer
That calls to Him - with honest faith -
To take us in His care
And - then - He will make light the ways
To what He, now, denies
And we will never fall again
Or have the need to cry.

Michael Dubina

. . . blessed are they that have not seen and have believed.
John 20:29

I Have No Worries

I have no worries of this world,
Not one uncertain time,
No moments of anxiety,
No obstacles to climb.

I place my daily trials aside
For Jesus to repair,
His sacrifice was cure alone
For burden we must bear.

So worry not for worldly things
And things that do not last,
But say instead a prayer
Of thanks that all these things
have passed.

Rick Hendrickson

The Guardian

He guards us through the dark of night
And shields us from temptation's dread -
Surrounds us with His healing light
And gives us promised peace instead.

He cares! Our Lord does truly care
About the trials we face on earth
And though we cannot see Him there
He fills us with a sense of worth.

If only we would try to hear
The calming comfort of His voice,
In quiet times, to feel Him near
We'd sing hosannas and rejoice.

For though our days are often tried
And pain portends a twilight dim,
To realize He's by our side
Makes life worth living, if lived for Him.

Polly Thornton

Peace

I find a peace with nature
Within the great outdoors,
Where trees grow tall - no fence - no wall -
The tide that finds the shore,
A forest deep that beckons me
A quiet country lane,
Blue skies above - a world of love
And gentle Springtime rain.

My heart finds peace when robins sing
Where little violets grow,
Neath Summer sun - where streamlets run
When Winter brings the snow.
So much of beauty is my own
Whatever time of year,
I find it all - the Spring - the Fall
And moments filled with cheer.

So many blessings day by day
The happiness I share,
The clouds on high - a breeze to sigh
A magic everywhere,
Because my mind finds things worthwhile
God's wondrous sweet release,
Each shining smile makes life worthwhile
And lends a lasting peace.

Garnett Ann Schultz

Grace and peace to you
through the knowledge
of God and of Christ, Jesus,
our Lord . . .
2 Pet. 1:2

In Perfect Harmony

What better scene to rest the soul
than boy and dog on grassy knoll
looking out across the vale,
with smiling face and wagging tail?
I lived my childhood Summers thus
with this fast friend I well could trust,
walking through the meadow green
beside a rambling brook of dreams.
And when we tired, we would rest
beneath a tree with redbird's nest
until we felt an urge to rove
and ramble through a singing grove.
No happier times have come my way
than those of bygone Summer days
that always ended far too soon,
there simply, purely was not room
to do the many things we planned,
but, then, tomorrow was at hand
when on our way we'd go again.
The years have come, the years have passed,
and often has my mind been cast
unto those precious days of yore
when my dog waited at the door.
O make me, God, a child again.
When mortal day has reached its end,
may my prayer to Thee ascend
to meet with Thine divine consent
. . . and Eternity with my friend, be spent.

Don Beckman

Hang Gliding

I think a window in the sky
Has opened on this place,
To let the eagles soaring by
See my astonished face.

The feel of being near to God,
To reach out for His hand,
And go where angels dare to trod,
Almost to Promised Land.

To glide above my human fear,
To trail where eagles fly,
How great to see the sun, up here,
Polishing God's sky.

It's if I fly with spirit wings,
Above the surly sod,
Race with a soaring wind that brings
Me here, closer to God.

Mary Dalton Crump

All of Me

Lord, I give You all of me;
Take me as I am.
Mold and shape each part You see,
To fit me in Your plan.
I'm Your willing servant, Lord,
To do as You command,
For I give You all of me;
My life is in Your hands.

Take me to a desert land,
Or lead me to the sea,
Away on some far distant shore,
Or in this land of free...
O'er mountains or in valleys,
'Neath skies of blue or gray,
Lord, I give You all of me,
So lead me in Your Way.

Grant, I pray Thee, this request:
Wouldst be my heart's content,
That I could be Your servant, Lord,
And go where I am sent.
I ask of nothing more, than of
Your face each day to see,
And one day hear You say, "Well done,
Child, you gave all to Me."

D. Sue Jones Horton

"If any man serve Me, let him follow Me;
and where I am, there shall also My servant be.
If any man serve Me, him will My Father honor."
John 12:26

Thanksgiving Day in the Country

There's a house in the country long miles away -
and it seems like a lifetime ago -
where our loved ones would gather on Thanksgiving Day
amid fields often "feathered" with snow.

We'd see the chimney's smoke curl to the skies
as we journeyed around the last bend;
the lights in the windows were welcoming eyes
and the porch like the arm of a friend!

Then mother and father, a little more grey,
would gaily greet all at the door,
and the house would soon echo with children at play
and a family together once more!

The aromas of turkey and dressing would fill
the rooms with their glorious smell
and we knew we would dine "divinely" until
our lives were replenished as well!

But first, heads were bowed for a moment of prayer
that father would lovingly give
in thanks for the blessings that all of us share
in this land where we freely may live!

As the hours sped by, and the flames flickered low
from the logs in the warm fireplace,
we knew it was time to reluctantly go
and we kissed every dear person's face!

And mother and father would wave from the door
as we "honked" last goodbyes from our cars,
then started the drive to our own homes once more
with our memories bright as the stars!

Now it seems that sometimes we can actually see
the light from their mansion above;
may the Family of Man some day be as free
to feast at God's banquet of love!

John C. Bonser

Sunshine in My Heart

However fretful or how blue,
My heavenly Father sees me through;
For if I act at His command,
He keeps me in His loving hand.

He always knows when things go wrong,
And fills my saddened heart with song;
However great may be my pain,
My Father makes me smile again!

He sends down blessings from above,
And warms me with His precious love;
Thus doleful be the day or dark,
There's sunshine in my happy heart!

Sancie Earman King

God's Majesty

Ah, Lord, how great Your majesty
In crimson leaves upon a tree -
More beauty than a heart can hold
On Autumn mornings, misted gold!

Ah, Lord, how great Your splendor, too,
In Summer roses kissed with dew!
Were I a queen upon a throne,
No greater treasure could I own.

Ah, Lord, how glorious Your morn
When Spring is suddenly reborn,
As purple crocus beckon me
Behold a world bejeweled by Thee.

And, Lord, how very kind art Thou
To mound soft snowflakes on the bough
So Winter's harshness we can bear
With ermine's magic everywhere.

In Summer, Autumn, Winter, Spring,
There's beauty in the smallest thing,
Reflecting Your great majesty,
Unfolding till eternity.

Sandra Town Lytle

The Prayer Flower

While walking through a forest
on the mountain top today,
I looked beside a solemn birch
and saw a flower pray.
All alone it bowed its head;
with none but me to see
the total reverence it expressed,
I wondered, could it be
that anyone in this cold world
would deep and truly care
enough about our loving God
for such perpetual prayer?
It really made me stop and think
a thought of soulful kind:
life will bloom the brighter
with God foremost in our mind.

Don Beckman

Quietude

I love the hours of quietude
I spend on hilltops high,
To marvel at life's peacefulness
Beneath a bright blue sky,
Perhaps to spend an hour in thought
Sometimes a magic dream,
And listen to the sighing breeze
Within this wondrous scene.

Sometimes a special quietude
Beside life's restless sea,
To capture all the miracles
In quiet reverie,
The calm I feel within my soul
Such fascination rare,
Enchanted by the wonderment
I'm ever finding there.

All nature seems to fondly lend
A soft and tender touch,
The mystery of life so dear
That always means so much,
A country lane - a meadow vast -
One special interlude,
The happiness that is my own
In hours of quietude.

Garnett Ann Schultz

For a Brand-New Day

Thank You, God, for a brand-new day;
And thank You for the chance to say
Those loving words that yesterday
I left unsaid, and went my way.
Thank You, God, for a brand-new day.
For showing me a better way
To share Your love and kindness show
So folk may see in me Your glow.
Thank You, God, for a brand-new day.
Be skies bright blue or stormy grey
Whatever comes is sent by You,
And by Your grace I'll make it through.
Thank You, God, for a brand-new day.
I will rejoice and not dismay.
I will be glad and lift above
My heart's praise for Your wondrous love.
Thank You, God, for a brand-new day.
May I cherish it, God, I pray;
And hear me as again I say:
Thank You, God, for a brand-new day!

Beverly J. Anderson

Smile

The thing that goes the farthest toward
Making life worthwhile,
That costs the least and does the most,
Is just a pleasant smile.
The smile that bubbles from a heart
That loves its fellow men,
Will drive away the clouds of gloom,
And coax the sun again;
It's full of worth and goodness, too,
With manly kindness blent,
It's worth a million dollars, and
It doesn't cost a cent.
There is no room for sadness
When we see a cheery smile
It always has the same good look -
It's never out of style;
It nerves us on to try again
When failure makes us blue,
The dimples of encouragement
Are good for me and you;
It pays a higher interest
For it is merely lent,
It's worth a million dollars and
It doesn't cost a cent.
A good thing to remember
And a better thing to do
To work with the construction gang
And with the wrecking crew.

The Lord is my light . . .
the Lord is the strength of my life . . .
whom shall I fear?
Ps. 27:1

We Can't . . .
but God Can!

Why things happen as they do
We do not always know,
And we cannot always fathom
Why our spirits sink so low . . .
We flounder in our dark distress,
We are wavering and unstable,
But when we're most inadequate
The Lord God's always able,
For though we are incapable,
God's powerful and great,
And there's no darkness of the mind
That God can't penetrate . . .
And all that is required of us
Whenever things go wrong
Is to trust in God implicitly
With a faith that's deep and strong,
And while He may not instantly
Unravel all the strands
Of the tangled thoughts that trouble us
He completely understands . . .
And in His time, if we have faith,
He will gradually restore
The brightness to our spirit
That we've been longing for.
So remember, there's no cloud too dark
For God's light to penetrate,
If we keep on believing
And have faith enough to wait!

Helen Steiner Rice

Leave Everything in God's Hands

Leave everything in God's hands.
The lilies do, you know.
Through sunshine and through darkness
The lilies grow.

Through cold and windy weather,
Through Winter's ice and snow
The lilies sleep in God's care...
Once more to grow.

In Spring they rise in beauty -
'Neath golden sun they glow;
And nourished by Spring showers
The lilies grow.

Leave everything in God's hands.
You're still more dear, you know,
Than all the blooming lilies
In fields that grow.

Oh, how you matter to Him.
He cares and loves you so;
He knows in shadowed valleys
Sweet virtues grow.

Yes, God knows all your needs, friend.
Seek Him in prayer. He'll show
In His time wondrous blessings.
He's promised so.

Leave everything in God's hands.
Trust Him Who loves you so.
For you are precious to Him.
You are, you know.

Beverly J. Anderson

Seasons of Life

Remember, though the season be
A blackish-gray monotony
Of cloudy sky and muffled sound
And snow that lies on frigid ground,

To each of us there comes a season
That soothes the soul and rights the reason,
When we have learned to cast aside
Our bitterness, our greed and pride.

And in their stead, we then displace
These senseless faults with God's pure grace
Then Winter's bitter wind departs
And we feel Spring within our hearts

Where flowers bloom in grand array
And rainbows chase the gloom away
For kinder thoughts and nobler deeds
Are what an ailing body needs.

At times we grow; at times we rest.
The time for each, He knows the best.
Through every season, oh may we be
Drawn closer Lord, my God, to Thee.

Polly Thornton

To everything there is a season,
and a time to every purpose
under the heaven . . .
Eccl. 3:1

The Source of Every Blessing

The source of every blessing
Is God, Who reigns above;
A God of love and mercy
And never failing love.

He blesses us with sunshine
And rain to make things grow,
He is there in Autumn's colors
And in Winter's falling snow.

He is there when health is failing
And burdens seem too hard to bear;
He reaches out with arms of love,
With compassion and infinite care.

To all who come unto Him,
He will never turn away,
To all who seek for mercy,
He is just a prayer away.

Frances Culp Wolfe

For with You
is the fountain of life,
and in Your light
we see light.
Ps. 37:10

It Will Always Be Amazing

It will always be amazing
How God loved and cared for me
When I had no time to listen
As He tried to speak to me.

I was young and very foolish
As I went my self-willed way.
Still He blessed me with His mercies,
And watched over me each day.

And He never loved me less, He
Just seemed to love me more,
Waiting patiently for me, to
Let Him enter my heart's door.

Then one day I felt so lonely
And I turned to God above.
Trusting Jesus as my Saviour,
I found God's redeeming love.

It will always be amazing
His forgiveness, oh, so sweet,
And my emptiness He filled with
Wondrous peace and joy complete.

Now for years we've walked together.
He's the dearest Friend to me.
There in gladness and in sadness
By my side He'll ever be.

It will always be amazing,
God's unfailing love and grace,
And one day in Heaven's glory
I'll behold Him face to face.

Beverly J. Anderson

A Faith Is Mine

A faith is mine because I know
The Spring will come - the grass will grow,
And Winter snow will melt away
Upon a lovely April day,
The earth will warm - trees burst in bloom
While nature sings a happy tune.

A faith is mine - the sun will rise
All golden in the eastern skies,
While gentle rain will bless the earth
In tender moments of rebirth,
And mountains tall will ever stand
To add a beauty to our land.

Somehow a quiet fills my heart
In joys and gladness life impart,
Believing - courage - each my own
In moments that I spend alone,
A world so filled with dreams divine
That will come true - a faith is mine.

Garnett Ann Schultz

God, Show Me How

God, give me wisdom to discern
Just where I am most needed
And grant nobody's cry for help
To me, shall go unheeded.
Let me see into those hearts
Who hide their deepest pain
And show me how to write the words
To bring them hope again.
Lord, You have given me so much
And now I want to share
The Love with which You shower me,
With people everywhere.
Though I brought nothing to this world
And that is how I'll leave it,
May all my poems ring out with Faith,
. . . The way that I believe it.

Grace E. Easley

Wisdom is a tree of life to those who grasp her, and he is happy who holds her fast.
Prov. 3:18

With Sled in Tow

It's Wintertime! The snow comes down
On country lanes, on streets in town;
With dazzling coats of pristine white
It blankets everything in sight;

And takes me back so long ago
When leaden skies brought our first snow
We raced to slopes of nearby hills
And with delight we took our spills

And sledded 'til the sun went down
Behind the mountains far from town.
Then in the evening's afterglow,
We plodded home, our sleds in tow.

I'll dream a dream of wintry eve
When I shall take my sled and leave
My fireside warmth for childhood thrills
On snow-clad slopes of nearby hills.

And Winter comes with its first snow -
I'll be a child with sled in tow.

Henry W. Gurley

Prayer for Strength

Give me strength of heart, Lord Jesus,
To endure the trials of time;
Give me strength of will and purpose
To pursue what is divine;
Give me strength of love and mercy
To forgive my fellowman
And the strength of truer wisdoms
To perceive and understand.
Give me greater strength of courage
That will better challenge strife;
Greater strength of faith and vision
To avoid the sins of life;
Give me strength of limb and body -
Strength to rise and build, anew -
And a strength that never wavers
In my trust and love for You.

Michael Dubina

Innocence

I saw the children playing
And how it brought to me,
The days when I was young and small
And from every heartache, free.

I held not then a troubling thought,
All of my days were full and free
And how my mind meandered back -
How those days were all for me.

Such innocence did so exist
So easily those days,
Chaste in that phase, the youth of life,
In oh, so many ways.

And I said a little prayer to God
To take my soul, back then,
And make me pure and whole and clean
As if, I were a child again.

James Joseph Huesgen

Faith Produces Works

Think of all God's done for us,
For, oh, it has been much;
He has provided every need...
Our raiment, food and such.
Through every valley He was there
To lift us mountain-high;
Whatever trials came our way,
He was the Light to guide.

Since God has done so much for us,
What have we done for Him?
He's given to us His only Son
To die for all our sins.
He asks nought else but this one thing...
That on Christ we believe,
But when we truly love the Lord,
Our faith will bring forth deeds.

Loise Pinkerton Fritz

Even so faith, if it hath not works,
is dead, being alone.
James 2:17

Growing in Grace

It took awhile for me to see
that no one's life is trouble free!
What must be done when fortune frowns?
Face it square on solid ground!

From God's own word I'm firmly told,
be ye brave and be ye bold;
Take a stand and stem the tide,
of hopeless thoughts - in faith abide.

God's faithfulness to me and you -
is really what will see us through!
No matter where in life we stand -
we're held securely in His hand.

It may not seem that He is there,
when we are visited by despair -
But heavenly hosts and angels near,
prevail upon us not to fear.

Unseen strength be yours and mine,
living life one day at a time -
Tomorrow may come - may stay away,
but we have in hand, the gift of today!

Janice C. Wright

*This is the day
the Lord has made;
Let us rejoice and
be glad in it.*
Ps. 118:24

Keep the Faith

Help us, Lord, to keep the faith
when things are going wrong...
Teach us to turn the other cheek
and move by faith along.

Just being good is not enough
while trying hard to cope.
We must put our faith to work
with charity and hope.

We need not fear the great unknown
when God is on our side,
And there is nothing we can't do
when faith in Him's applied!

There is no power on this earth
that's worthy of our fear,
For Christ shall send a Comforter
to believers far and near.

Help us, Lord, to keep the faith
and never turn away...
Show us, Lord, Thy majesty;
abide with us today.

Clay Harrison

*Now faith is the substance
of things hoped for,
the evidence of
things not seen.*
Heb. 11:1

Shelter Us

With happy hearts and hymns of praise
We ask You bless our earthly days -
We ask You guide in all we do,
Make us humble, kind and true.

God, shelter us in Your strong arms.
Let us be free and safe from harm,
And when we wander, rein us in
To Your sheltering arms again.

Gertrude Blau Byram

God's Rebel Rose

It clings, tenacious, to the vine
Where, once, it bloomed
and reigned, sublime -
And snows of Winter, sleet and hail,
Cannot upon its will prevail.

One Rebel Rose - long past its prime -
Still clings onto its mother vine
And scorns the rule that it comply
With nature's law to fall and die.

Michael Dubina

Texture of My Soul

May the texture of my soul
Be as fine as it can be;
May it be the kind of texture
That greatly pleases Thee.
May not a thread of coarseness
Be any part of it,
But only finest woven threads
That for my King are fit.

May the texture of my soul
Be as Thou would have it be;
May it e'er be interwoven
With threads of purity.
Threads of faith, forgiveness, love,
Humbleness of mind;
Then may the texture of my soul
Be fully holy-lined.

Loise Pinkerton Fritz

Because it is written,
"Be ye holy; for I am holy."
I *Peter* 1:16

Nobody's Perfect

Nobody's perfect, all of us have
Traits we must overcome,
Regrets for the things it is too
late to change,
For what we have not, or have done.
But we just have to do the best
that we can,
Believing that God will come through,
And if we fall down, we must get
up again,
The way that He wants us to do.
For nobody's perfect, once there
was One,
Born in a stable dim,
Sinless and blameless, Whose message
was Love,
. . . But the people crucified Him!

Grace E. Easley

Early Spring

I love these days in early Spring
When hills are turning green,
And every leaf and blade of grass
Is bathed with dewy sheen.
There is no need for coaxing
To leave behind the chores,
On slightest pretense I am quick
To wander out-of-doors.
I love the tang of Springtime air
Brimful with blossoms sweet;
A carpet made of lush green grass
Springs softly 'neath our feet.
Within my neighbor's garden near
Bright daffodils now bloom
And from my window I can hear
A robin's cheery tune.
These are the days I cherish most
When birds come back to sing,
And everywhere God seems to say:
Come, say "hello" to Spring!

Kay Hoffman

It's April

It's April and once more I see
New leaf and bud on greening tree,
The flowers rising from the sod
And opening petaled eyes to God;
Again, the earth is sparkling clean
And dressed in Springtime's apple-green.

It's April and once more I hear
The robin's trill so sweet and clear,
The brooks' and streamlets' merry song
As freed from ice they roll along;
Again, young bleating lambs at play
Are heard in meadows 'cross the way.

It's April and once more I know
The warmth that comes from Springtime's glow,
The hope that's in my heart reborn
With every shining April morn;
Again, I know God's promise true...
To all things He gives life anew!

Beverly J. Anderson

The Journey Home

Don't worry about anything,
For don't you know it's true,
A loving God has launched the ship
That gently carries you.

Each boat that sails the sea of life
That rocks with every storm,
Is guided through the straits of faith
To a harbor safe and warm.

The Hand that knit you in the womb
Will never cease to care,
A ballast in the wildest wind
A love that's always there.

For no one lives but by His grace
And given is each breath,
Well known the time of every birth
The hour of every death.

And each man hears a special call
That beckons him alone,
While God provides along the way
The stars that guide him home.

Kate Watkins Furman

Slow Me Down

Lord, slow me down!
I need to pause
And watch the butterfly,
Behold the trees
Waft in the breeze
And hear a baby's cry.
Give me the time,
The time to see
How Your creations praise Your name.
From sky to sea
Your Majesty
They openly proclaim.
Yes, slow me down
That I may see
Exactly how it's done.
Then, may I, too,
With nature's crew
Worship You through Your Son.

Janice George

And he said unto them,
"Come ye yourselves apart
into a desert place,
and rest a while . . ."
Mark 6:31

God's Gift of Memory

We can't bring back the good old days,
For they're now past; they're gone.
We can't reverse the days of time,
They just keep marching on.
We only have the present day,
Perhaps the future, too,
But God has never promised us
Another day we'd view.

We can't bring back the good old days,
Not in reality,
But we can still catch glimpses
Through eyes of memory.
We can't bring back those cherished times
But they can come to us,
For through God's gift of memory,
They still our hearts can touch.

Loise Pinkerton Fritz

Whereas ye know not what
shall be on the morrow.
For what is your life?
It is even a vapour,
that appeareth for a little time,
and then vanisheth away.
James 4:14

A Wealth of Memories

My heart is full as I recall
A wealth of memories,
Which can cheer my lonely days
And put my heart at ease.

My mind goes back to Mama
And a gentle, loving Dad,
A Grandma sweet and tender
And a dog that we called "Chad."

Faithful friends were cherished
And held in high esteem;
You greeted each tomorrow
As you dared to dream your dream.

Life was plainly simple,
Devoid of fear and hate,
When love of God or country
Were not up for debate.

If everyone would realize
How precious life can be,
They'd care for one another
And sweet memories achieve.

Catherine Janssen Irwin

One Little Stray

Out in the pasture, the sheep lay 'round
Quiet and tranquil, not making a sound.
When one little sheep, 'twas not very old
Got up from the flock, strayed out in the cold.

For many a year, he wandered afar
Mid turmoil, he hungered, felt thorns that did scar,
Over rocky roads that were rough and steep,
Carrying a memory, in his heart, so deep.

The loving Shepherd left His flock one day,
Went out to the desert to find His stray.
At last, He heard the little one's cry -
He found him helpless, about to die.

On shoulders strong, He carried His own,
From ninety-nine others, no more will he roam.
The angels in heaven rejoiced 'round the throne,
For the Good Shepherd had brought
His lost one back home.

Darlene LaRose Skiff

World of Chapels

There's a church, around the corner,
That I visit every day,
But it's not the only chapel
Where I choose to kneel and pray,
For I pray, in different places -
When I feel the need for prayer -
And the Lord is always with me,
Does not matter when or where.
So, the church - around the corner -
Is a special place to me,
But it's not the only chapel
Where I know the Lord to be,
For I find Him, always waiting -
Anywhere I choose to pray -
In my world of many chapels
That I enter every day.

Michael Dubina

Treasures I Hold Dear

My days are filled with treasured things
From dawn of morning's light
To sunset when the shadows fall
To bring the welcomed night.

The treasure of a loyal friend...
The treasure of a smile...
The treasure of another day
To make it all worthwhile.

The treasure of a solid faith
To make my world grow bright...
The treasure that He guides my steps
From dawn to sunset's flight...

My days, of course, are centered on
This thing called "life's career,"
But in pursuit of long-sought dreams,
I hold these treasures dear.

Henry W. Gurley

The Ecstasies of Spring

I am old, and yet I know
the ecstasies of Spring -
The joy of budding roses
and bluebirds on the wing.

My heart is almost glowing
to see the rivers run,
And there's comfort just in knowing
there will be morning sun.

The cold, white shawl of Winter
once more is packed away
As the creatures of the forest
come again to play.

Each garden is a showplace -
a masterwork of art.
For the ecstasies of Spring
have blossomed in my heart.

Clay Harrison

Great and wonderful are your works, Lord God almighty . . .
Rev. 15:3

Home and Hearth

Home and hearth, such sweet words,
I ponder in my muse,
For they tell of simple joys,
The ones I do most choose . . .
For home's a cheery haven
With hearth so red aglow,
Where cares are oft' unburdened
And peace is good to know . . .
The dearest place upon the earth,
A respite from the storm,
Where hearts are sharing kinship
And building memories warm . . .
Home and hearth, such sweet words,
They signify true rest,
Where life's simple pleasures
Are at their very best!

Virginia Borman Grimmer

Time for God

At the end of the day when the world is still
And my thoughts can return to memory,
I like to relax by my windowsill
And watch the great river glide out to sea.
It ripples along in an easy way,
As the lights blink on shining streaks of gold,
Across sparkling water for sun's last ray -
Just a final gleam as the day grows old.

Serenity comes to my window seat...
It's peaceful and calm as I linger there.
This hour of rest has become my retreat;
A place for solace and freedom from care.
Each of us seeks out a place he can be
Closer to God and tranquility.

Marian Ford Park

Cabin of My Dreams

There is a cabin of my dreams
To which I often go,
Sometimes amid the Autumn leaves
Or nestled in the snow.
It's close beside a crystal stream,
Wherein I often swim,
And there are deer who never mind
That I am watching them.
There is a cabin of my dreams,
Rustic, quaint and small,
And yet I feel when I am there
I surely have it all.
It has two ample windows
Through which the sunlight streams,
And when dusk falls, the honeysuckle
Drifts into my dreams.

There is no need to lock the door,
No one lives out this far,
And I do very well indeed
Without a bus or car.
I've spent some happy hours
On that bench beneath the trees,
My homemade bread is sweetened
With wild honey from the bees.
Because one cannot see it
Doesn't mean it isn't there,
It is my secret refuge
From a world so full of care.
Within its walls an atmosphere
Of true simplicity,
And we are one, who dwell within,
. . . My little dog and me.

Grace E. Easley

If Memories Are Riches

I'll always have my memories,
When I am old and gray,
And they at least are something
No one can take away.
I could not ask for greater wealth,
Because they are so dear
And I will never wish for more
As long as I am here.
For if they measure riches by
Memories here on earth,
I'll surely be a millionaire -
So great would be their worth.

Harold F. Mohn

I Thank God for My Home

When sunrise lights the morning skies
Over our village paradise
And roosters crow their "wake-up" call
For us to hear, both one and all,
I thank God for my home.
It's not a palace for a king;
It's just a country cottage, small,
But, oh, the joys it ever brings,
Joys nestled there within its walls.
Here family lives with God as guide;
Here love for one another reigns.
All things are taken in their stride;
Concern for each one never wanes.
The windowsills hold flowers, bright,
That shed a ray of welcome here
And beckon to the flowers outside,
The gardens with their floral cheer.
When sunup fills the earthen floor
And touches on each village door
And folks begin their work each day
In their same good old-fashioned way,
I thank God for my home.

Loise Pinkerton Fritz

. . . but as for me and my house,
we will serve the Lord.
Joshua 24:15

Holy
Is His Name

Through the many, many years
There are many smiles and tears;
Yet the smiles predominate
If we live for Jesus' sake.

Tho the years may heartaches bring;
Yet the heart shall surely sing;
If to Jesus we belong,
For His very name is song.

Saviour hear me, as I pray,
That I dedicate each day
To Thy precious Holy Name;
Which is evermore the same!

Sancie Earman King

Time for Change

When our hair has turned to silver
And our steps are slowed by years
We must change our style of living -
In some ways we don't endear;
Younger hands must do the planting;
Stronger hearts must run the race;
You and I must love, more dearly,
While we 'wait the Lord's embrace.

It is time for little diversions,
From our ways of younger years;
Time to live with limitations
Greying years combined with fears;
Younger hands must cut the timber;
Stronger hearts must climb the hill;
You and I must dress, more warmly,
To endure each Winter's chill.

We must, also, pray to Jesus
For the comforts of His love
To sustain us and endear us
For Eternity, above;
Younger hands must do the labors;
Stronger hearts must lead the chase;
You and I must love, more dearly,
While we 'wait the Lord's embrace.

Michael Dubina

I Offer Thanks

I offer thanks for friends so dear,
For every word of joy and cheer,
The quiet moments I so love
And blue skies there so high above,
The special dreams that are my own
And every beauty I have known.

I offer thanks for Springtime days
And happiness on country ways,
The precious laughter of a child
And tiny violets growing wild,
The brook that murmurs as it flows,
The magic of a Junetime rose.

For sun and rain and gentle earth
The miracle of Spring's rebirth,
Each Autumn color bright and bold,
For snowflakes soft and Winter's cold,
The sea that rushes to its banks,
For God and love - I offer thanks.

Garnett Ann Schultz

Lack of Knowledge

When I was young I wondered how
the sky could be so blue;
what kept the clouds from falling down,
why four was two times two?

I asked my elders why green leaves
should turn to browns and reds,
and they would often frown at me
or shake impatient heads

and say "when you are older, lad,
you'll understand such things,
and know the reason snow is white
and why a bird has wings."

Yet, I am older now and find
when children question me
that it is hard to answer them
and not speak foolishly.

For this is truth: the questions asked
are quite profound and wise;
it only is in adult minds
the lack of knowledge lies!

John C. Bonser

The Little Horse Who Failed

Once there was a little horse
who entered in a race,
but due to careless folly
it ended in disgrace.

This came about when he outran
the others on the track
so far, he wondered where they were
and took a quick glance back.

When he stopped, the second horse
the turf did swiftly spin,
and with his four hoofs flying,
beat him to the win.

So let this be a lesson:
run your race in your own time
and regarding competition,
never stop to look behind.

For we are individuals;
with ourselves we must compete,
and to concentrate on rivals
is to suffer sure defeat.

Don Beckman

Admonition

Reach out your hand to those in need,
Say not, "I have no time to give,"
True joy is in the kindly deed,
And peace is in the love we live.

Be fond of virtue more than gold,
Let blessed truth be in your heart;
Onto the right path firmly hold
And vanquish evil from the start.

The God of Wisdom has a plan,
And to this plan all things are bound.
His gift of freedom is, for man,
The greatest treasure to be found.

We have this life in which to live
Our freedom choices day to day:
It's not to evil we should give
Our very souls and lives away!

George R. Kossik

Then Jesus approached and said to them,
"All power in heaven and
on earth has been given to Me.
Go, therefore, and make disciples of all nations,
baptizing them in the name of the Father,
and of the Son, and of the Holy Spirit . . ."
Matt. 28:18-20

The Great Commission

It's not hard to be a Christian
and fill a friendly pew
Where only friends surround you
and praise the things you do.
But God would have us share His word
with those who know Him not
On darkened streets and avenues
where sinners cast their lot.

Here dwell the non-believers,
and those who have not heard
That Jesus Christ still loves them
according to His word.
Here dwell the lost and lonely,
the homeless and the proud,
Who, like sheep, have gone astray
by following the crowd.

Here dwell the broken-hearted,
the abandoned and abused,
Who have seen the "Sunday Christians"
and walked away confused.
It's not hard to be a Christian
and fill a friendly pew,
But after the Benediction...
can Christ be found in you?

Clay Harrison

*"Go ye therefore,
and teach all nations . . ."*
Matt. 28:19

After the Winter, God Sends the Spring

Springtime is a season
Of hope and joy and cheer.
There's beauty all around us
To see and touch and hear.
So, no matter how downhearted
And discouraged we may be,
New hope is born when we behold
Leaves budding on a tree,
Or when we see a timid flower
Push through the frozen sod
And open wide in glad surprise
Its petaled eyes to God,
For this is just God saying,
"Lift up your eyes to Me,
And the bleakness of your spirit,
Like the budding Springtime tree,
Will lose its wintry darkness
And your heavy heart will sing" -
For God never sends the Winter
Without the joy of Spring.

Helen Steiner Rice

Get Away from All of It

Sometimes I surely think that I
Would like to get away
From all of it and be alone
And rest and think and pray.

I could relax and contemplate
The joys that I have had
And I could read some Scripture for
It makes one's heart so glad.

'Twould also serve to brush away
The cobwebs from my mind,
'Twould help me to make light my load
And leave my cares behind.

In fact I think that ev'ryone
Should sometimes get away
From all of it and contemplate,
Relax and think and pray.

Luther Elvis Albright

Persevere in prayer,
and watch in
it with thanksgiving.
Col. 4:2

Autumn

Amber, crimson, russet, gold,
Foliage colors now unfold.
Bright the sky and crisp the air,
Signs of Autumn everywhere.

Orange pumpkins in the field,
Harvest shows a lavish yield.
Roadside stands are quite a treat
Laden with good things to eat.

Scarlet sumac are ablaze
All along the country ways;
Goldenrod and asters, too,
Lend their charm for us to view.

Autumn calls the heart to praise
For the bounty of Fall days,
For the beauty we behold
When the leaves turn red and gold.

Beverly J. Anderson

And he changeth
the time and
the season . . .
Dan. 2:21

Set Me Afire

Lord, set me afire with a white-hot blaze,
Consuming all of my willful ways,
Burn away all that You see,
That might deter or hinder me.
Sear me right down to the bone,
'Til every sinful thought is gone,
Let the flames rise hot and bright,
Like a scarlet vigil light.

Lord, let me mirror only Thee,
'Til there's nothing left of me,
Let my soul reflect the glow
Of Thy goodness here below.
Rid me of each vain desire,
In this ever-cleansing fire,
And when my heart shall cease to beat,
. . . Bless these ashes at Thy feet.

Grace E. Easley

A Day Worthwhile

I count that day as wisely spent
In which I do some good
For someone who is far away
Or shares my neighborhood.
A day devoted to the deed
That lends a helping hand
And demonstrates a willingness
To care and understand.
I long to be of usefulness
In little ways and large
Without a selfish motive
And without the slightest charge.
Because in my philosophy
There never is a doubt
That all of us here on earth
Must help each other out.
I feel that day is fruitful
And the time is worth the while
When I promote the happiness
Of one enduring smile.

My Daily Prayer

Give me a spirit sweet, dear Lord,
As I go about my day,
That I would be a blessing glad
To someone on life's way.
Let no small pettiness of mine
Keep me from doing good,
To help where there's a need, and love
My neighbor as I should.
When I would seek my will, not Yours,
Speak to my heart anew;
Give me a vision clear, dear Lord,
Of what You'd have me do.
Please grant to me the strength I need
To stand for right and good,
Rememb'ring that we all should strive
To do the things You would.
Lord, let me not be boastful of
Some good that I have done,
But keep me ever mindful that
From You my blessings come.
I do not ask for riches grand,
Nor skies forever fair;
A closer walk with You, dear Lord,
This is my daily prayer.

Kay Hoffman

Gentle Folk

Sometimes it so amazes me,
The love that people give,
They lighten up my darkest hours
And help my soul to live.

Just when I'm feeling down
At times, a friend appears
To put a smile inside my heart,
And wipe away my tears.

It makes me realize how much God
Loves us through and through,
When He takes the time to care for me
Through gentle folk like you.

James Joseph Huesgen

The Secret

I met God in the morning
When my day was at its best,
And His presence came like sunrise,
Like a glory in my breast.
All day long the Presence lingered,
All day long He stayed with me,
And we sailed in perfect calmness
O'er a very troubled sea.
Other ships were blown and battered,
Other ships were sore distressed,
But the winds that seemed to drive them
Brought to us a peace and rest.
Then I thought of other mornings,
With a keen remorse of mind,
When I too had loosed the moorings,
With the Presence left behind.
So I think I know the secret,
Learned from many a troubled way:
You must seek Him in the morning
If you want Him through the day!

Ralph Spaulding Cushman

The Heralds of Spring

A nest and two birds in a tree,
Two birds singing merrily;
There'll soon be a family...
This is the sign of Spring.

Flow'rs peeking through snow-dusted ground,
Emerging without slightest sound,
Brightening the landscape around...
This is the sign of Spring.

A rainbow aglow in the sky
After a shower from on high,
A gorgeous sight to the eye...
This is the sign of Spring.

A branched pussy willow tree
With catkins so silvery,
A most welcome sight to see...
This is the sign of Spring.

The peepers a-peeping out yon
In woods at the set of sun,
All heralds of what has come...
Colorful, life-filled Spring.

Loise Pinkerton Fritz

Nevertheless he left not himself without witness, in that he did good, and gave us rain from heaven, and fruitful seasons, filling our hearts with food and gladness.
Acts 14:17

Snow Picnic

I planned a picnic in the snow,
Invited feathered friends I know.
I scattered crumbs and seeds to eat,
With suet for a special treat;

Then took my place at window seat,
Each honored guest to quietly greet.
Slate-colored juncos came to call
And brown-hued chipping sparrows small.

The cardinals perched on ice-white spread
In splendid coats of crimson red.
I watched the purple finches dine
In royal bibs, raspberry wine.

Towhee, nuthatch and chickadee
Had gracious manners one could see.
When kingly blue jay lit to taste,
The other birds made room in haste.

My friends chirped thanks for crisp birdfeed,
Nutritious food that filled each need.
I listened joyfully and thought
Of Winter wonder God's birds brought.

Louise Pugh Corder

Beside the Waters

Beside the quiet rippling streams
My Lord is leading me,
All nature bears His spoken word
In everything I see.
For lo, He comes to comfort me
And sits down at my side,
He whispers in the breezes
Blowing gently through my mind.
The waters ripple gently on,
So quiet and serene,
And on its waves I see His truth
Reflecting like a dream.

And mounted up on eagle's wings,
The Master makes me soar,
Above the waters running still
And all because He's Lord.
Reflected on the ripples are
The trees and skies above,
Resplendent with the sun,
As warm as God's abiding love.
A place where I find solitude
Without a single care,
Beside the waters deep and still,
My Father leads me there.

Thomas P. McHugh

. . . he leadeth me beside still waters.
He restoreth my soul . . .
Ps. 23:2-3

Beware the Seed

Beware! Beware
What seeds you sow
If - what they bear -
You do not know.
For, what you sow,
The Lord will grow
And you must harvest
What you sow.

Be sure,
Of what you want to grow
Above the earth
Or down, below;
And never sow
A bitter seed
That will but grow
A bitter weed.

Michael Dubina

. . . they that plow iniquity, and sow wickedness, reap the same.
Job 4:8

The Faith of a Mustard Seed

How often I have stumbled
along life's narrow way.
How often I have grumbled
at the first light of day.
When the road of life grows weary,
I want to run and hide,
When days are dark and dreary,
I lock myself inside.
In times of toil and trouble,
I often fail the test.
When misfortunes burst my bubble,
I'm seldom at my best.
When the storms of life assail me
and knock me to my knees,
I realize I could not see
the forest for the trees.
For God had always been there
waiting to meet my need,
And all I had to do was share
the faith of a mustard seed.

Clay Harrison

And the Lord said,
"If you have faith
the size of a mustard
seed you would
say to this tree, 'Be
uprooted and planted
in the Sea,' and it
would obey you."
Luke 17:6

Not by Chance nor Happenstance

Into our lives come many things
to break the dull routine,
The things we had not planned on
that happen unforeseen,
The unexpected little joys
that are scattered on our way,
Success we did not count on
or a rare, fulfilling day -
A catchy, lilting melody
that makes us want to dance,
A nameless exaltation
of enchantment and romance -
An unsought word of kindness,
a compliment or two
That sets the eyes to gleaming
like crystal drops of dew -

The unplanned sudden meeting
that comes with sweet surprise
And lights the heart with happiness
like a rainbow in the skies...
Now some folks call it fickle fate
and some folks call it chance,
While others just accept it
as pleasant happenstance -
But no matter what you call it
it didn't come without design,
For all our lives are fashioned
by the Hand that is divine -
And every happy happening
and every lucky break
Are little gifts from God above
that are ours to freely take.

Helen Steiner Rice

A New Beginning

With the newness of each morning
When the sun begins to rise,
How our hearts are filled with joy
As we gaze up to the skies.

For each dawn is filled with gladness
We're so grateful for the day,
One more chance to do God's bidding
And make amends for yesterday.

As we spend these precious hours
May we ever be aware
That this gift of one more day
Is but a gift to spend with care.

Every day's a new beginning,
Though the last it may well be,
But if we spend it well, we'll spend
Our life with Him eternally.

Polly Thornton

*. . . Amend your ways
and your deeds . . .*
Jer. 7:3

The Spring

There's a trail winds down from my house
to a lovely little spring
Where goldenrod grows all around
and pheasants take to wing;
Where bees buzz 'round wild flowers
of yellow, blue and white,
And hummingbirds and insects feed
as they move from site to site.

In Wintertime, when all is still
as a picture in a book,
My spring keeps on a-bubbling
to begin its little brook.
And then I know - no matter how
my world may rock and spin,
God is in His heaven, and
it will all come right again.

Frankie Davis Oviatt

The glory of life is to love,
not to be loved,
To give, not to get,
to serve, not to be served;
To be a strong hand in the dark
to another in time of need,
To be a cup of strength to
any soul in a crisis of weakness.
This is to know the glory of life.

The Eagle

Come walk with me today
Beneath God's bright blue sky,
See the eagle in the distance,
Ride the currents, gliding high.

Reaching upward, ever upward,
Almost disappear from view,
Then returning to her small ones
When the heat of day is through.

And I feel quite like the eagle
Flying high when all is well,
Never thinking of storms raging
In the sky and heart as well.

Your love is like the sun, my God,
That helps the eagle rise.
Without it in this world I know
We could never reach the sky.

We would always sit upon the rim,
And never dare to fly.
The valley then would be our home.
And happiness would die.

So always walk the world, my friend,
In the Sonshine of His love.
Don't sit upon the rim and dream,
Fly with eagles - high above.

Nancy Smith

Dear Friend . . .

Wait, reflect and pray, dear friend,
And Christ will give you love;
Reach out to Him Who brings you joy,
And blessings from above.

Wait, reflect and pray, dear friend,
And Christ will give you grace;
Come, tarry for a little while,
And rest in His embrace.

Wait, reflect and pray, dear friend,
And Christ will give you hope;
He'll help you strive to carry on,
And give you strength to cope.

Wait, reflect and pray, dear friend,
And Christ will give you life;
He'll be there ever by your side,
And take away your strife.

Wait, reflect and pray, dear friend,
And Christ will give you peace;
Remember Him when skies are dark,
And you will find release!

Hope C. Oberhelman

Before the Dawn of Day

Oh may I seek Thee, Father, God,
Before the dawn of day;
That I might find, through eyes of faith,
All cobwebs swept away.
If I have failed, in evening hours,
To do Thy perfect will;
Oh may I, God, come morning light,
My mission to fulfill!
Oh help me fathom, Father, God,
Thy bounties all around;
That I not cease to praise Thy name,
My joy in Thee abounds!
May I recall a special morn
When darkened were the skies;
When mammoth stone was rolled away,
As tears filled Mary's eyes!
For she heard Jesus call her name,
As none had done before,
And thus, tho dawn had not appeared,
The skies were dark no more!
My Heavenly Father, tho as yet
No sunlight gilds the skies;
Oh may I, God, through joy in Thee,
Be blest in Thy dear eyes!

Sancie Earman King

At the End of the Tunnel

There's a light at the end of the tunnel,
So courage, faint of heart
And somewhere in the darkest night,
A place where shadows part.
There's always a way, though I may not
Be able to see it now
And someday I will gather up,
All Heaven will allow.

There's a time of peace and plenty,
Though I struggle through today
And in His own good time, the Lord
Will take the hurt away,
For Paradise is waiting,
Beyond my span of years
And in the joy of loving,
I will forget my tears.

There's a light at the end of the tunnel,
Though there are miles to go,
My Lord will not forsake me,
For He has told me so.
And "all that eye has never seen,
And ear has never heard,"
One day He will present to me,
. . . Who take Him at His word.

Grace E. Easley

*. . . Eye hath not seen, nor ear heard,
neither have entered into the heart of man,
the things which God hath prepared
for them that love Him.*
1 Cor. 2:9

February Contentment

February's a respite
From Winter's normal pace.
The local world is snowbound.
Earth wears a frozen face.

Small seeds sleep under blankets
Of softest eiderdown.
Each evergreen is well-wrapped
In lacy shawl and gown.

Inside we pull our armchairs
Close to the fire's red gleam.
We share our treasured memories,
Plan Summer's garden, dream.

Though all outside is icy,
Inside there's warm content,
A gratitude for loved ones,
And peace that's heaven-sent.

Louise Pugh Corder

Beyond the Winter

Somewhere beyond the Winter
Awaits the magic Spring,
The miracle of sunshine
And robins on the wing,
When gentle April showers
Cleanse God's greening earth,
With streamlets flowing freely
In nature's bright rebirth.

Beyond the days of Winter
Beyond the ice and snow,
With blue skies high above us
While gentle breezes blow,
The miracle of Springtime
And blossoms bursting wide,
The loveliness of wildflowers
To bless the countryside.

The season of fulfillment
Each moment shining fair,
So many new tomorrows
Just nothing can compare,
A new world now unfolding
Dispelling Winter's gloom,
We look beyond the Winter
To Springtime's happy tune.

Garnett Ann Schultz

Beyond the Clouds

My precious Saviour, tho my cares
Come tumbling, crashing down,
I know that when I take Thy hand,
Bright sunlight shines around.
For Thou my Saviour, Who art God,
With Whom I'm yet in touch,
Oh, how can I explain Thy love,
Which brought me through so much?
For even tho the clouds be dense
And stormy be the sea,
I know that Thou canst still my soul,
Who silenced Galilee.
Thus, tho the clouds grow very dense
And cares seem not to cease,
I know my Saviour, only Thee,
Canst give to me Thy peace.

For how can I explain Thy love,
Which went to utmost length,
Whom, tho I'm weak and weary worn,
Canst give to me Thy strength.
And when I grow so very tired
That I can walk no more,
You carry me within Thine arms,
Thou Christ, Whom I adore.
For when You carry me my Lord,
By Whom the world was planned,
Along the shore can only see,
Thy footprints in the sand.
Oh Jesus, precious Saviour mine,
Who gave to me Thy grace,
I still can see, beyond the clouds,
The radiance of Thy face!

Sancie Earman King

A Fond Farewell

I have watched you gather, robins,
For your meeting of the clan;
To chirp a loud approval
Of this season's travel plan.

Just keep in mind, you wanderers,
As you dine here one last time,
How we waited your arrival
From that warm and sunny clime!

It is sad to bid you God-speed
As you leave our lawn today,
But chilling North winds warn us
That you must be on your way.

So, 'til Spring, safe journey, robins!
For it's comforting to know
You'll sing praise to your Creator -
No matter where you go.

Helen M. Motti

Retreat

Close out the world
And come to Me,
Distractions leave behind;
I am your life, your soul's sweet breath,
The healer of your mind.
Begin to know the meaning of
A secret place with Me;
I wait within your heart to hear
You praise Me joyfully.
I dwell within your inner court
And wait to speak with you,
To give direction to your life,
To guide in all you do.
Could you but understand, My child,
That though your heart seeks Me,
You are distracted by world's cares,
Breaking affinity...
To block communication, the messages I speak,
Please ponder this, for quiet time
Holds answers that you seek.
Draw not your own conclusions;
Put confidence in Me
Grow daily in obedience
To reach maturity.

Anna Lee Edwards McAlpin

When You Kneel to Pray

Our sad world needs a lift today;
Remember when you kneel to pray
To ask Our Blessed Lord, above,
To shed His mercy and His love.

Crime is rampant everywhere
And hard times have brought despair;
Dread diseases known to some
Can't easily be overcome.

The homeless line our city streets
And even the strong admit defeat;
Smiles are few and far between,
Life seems to have lost its sheen.

Drought and floods have left their mark
And our children fear the dark;
Wars which we can't understand
Wreak havoc on a foreign land.

Gloom and misery fill the air,
Non-believers fail to care;
Only God can end our plight,
So trust and pray with all your might.

Catherine Janssen Irwin

The Eagle's Flight

I saw the eagle mount the wind
And soar into the stormy sky,
Catching each gust with strong wing,
He let the storm lift him high
Above the craggy, snowcapped peak.
Unafraid, trusting the power within,
The might to soar and seek
Each updraft along the canyon rim,
To carry him ever higher.
Oh bird, you touched a troubled heart.
Your trust did my own inspire.
Even if the storms do not depart,
I've found within myself the power
To use the very storms of life
To surmount each dark hour,
Trust God, let the winds of strife
Or grief or fear not keep me low
But through faith, be a catalyst
To seek the heights I need to know
To make a better world and fears resist.

Minnie Boyd Popish

Lonesome

Dear Master, I am lonesome;
Dear Master, speak to me!
I've been longing here at twilight
For the voices o'er the sea,
And it seems as if my heartache
Would be hushed, less piercing be,
If Thou, Lord, wouldst come still closer -
I am lonesome; speak to me!
I've been thinking in the stillness,
As I've watched the sunset glow
Die out yonder on the hilltop,
Leaving naught but cold and woe -
I've been thinking of the faces
That have come a-trooping by,
Old-time faces, long-time vanished,
Leaving me to wait and sigh.
And I'm lonesome, Lord, I'm lonesome;
Come Thou closer; speak to me,
For I am listening here at twilight
To the voices o'er the sea,
And it seems as if my heartache
Would be hushed, less piercing be,
If Thou, Lord, wouldst come still closer -
I am lonesome; speak to me!

Ralph Spaulding Cushman

Listening Ears

To those of us who cannot hear
The songs that fill each day
Or hear the words of loving hearts
Who would enrich our way,
The joys of such - the Lord decrees -
No fate of life deny
So He bequeaths all deafened ears
The Grace of Listening Eyes.

Eyes that hear (through smiles and tears)
What deafened ears deny
And bring to heart the truths of life
That make us laugh or cry;
He coddles us - who cannot hear -
With mercies of His Grace
To let us hear - with Listening Eyes -
The joys that life embrace.

Michael Dubina

Ask Not What God Can Do for You

Ask not what God can do for you -
He does it every day,
From the first bright rays of sunlight
To moonlight on the bay.
Each day's another blessing -
Each season a delight,
For those who truly know Him
And walk within His light.
His love is everlasting -
His promises are true.
His children know already
What God can do for you.
His words are awe inspiring -
His gifts are free to all,
And He is always watching
Each time a sparrow falls.
He's the Alpha and Omega -
Creator of all men!
Ask not what God can do for you -
Believe and let Him in!

Clay Harrison